Groundbreaking ceremony 1915

As a San Diego native and one who has a deep appreciation for the unique beauty of Balboa Park, it gives me great pleasure to share Richard Benton's stunning photographic portrayal of our City's crown jewel.

I am reminded daily of how fortunate we are to have a place as special as Balboa Park in San Diego. As the Councilmember who is fortunate to have the Park included in my district, I often boast about its charm, beauty, and ambiance. San Diegans treasure the Balboa Park for its tranquil open spaces and lush gardens that are an oasis in the midst of our urban metropolis. We also cherish the history that is represented in the wonderful Spanish Colonial Revival architecture of the buildings constructed for the international expositions of 1915 and 1935. We take great pride in Balboa Park's internationally famous San Diego Zoo, as well as the renowned museums and institutions which help to create a cultural synergy that is unmatched anywhere.

Mr. Benton's photographs capture the majesty and magic of Balboa Park, demonstrating that the spirit of culture and beauty created in 1915 for the Panama-California Exposition is still alive and well today. I hope that you are inspired by this book and that you not only visit in person, but support the Park and its institutions so that this great civic treasure can continue to inspire for the next 100 years.

Council President Todd Gloria

Fewer than 40,000 citizens lived in the City of San Diego when planning began for the 1915-1916 Panama-California Exposition, which would forever change Balboa Park, and would alter the course of San Diego history—it was the most significant event ever to take place in San Diego. Citizens pledged their own money and many worked without pay to make the exposition a success, attracting more than three million visitors. When San Francisco was chosen to host the official world's fair, San Diegans forged ahead with an exposition unlike any that had come before, with its Spanish Colonial Revival architecture and beautiful gardens. The Exposition theme was the progress of mankind, demonstrated in the anthropological exhibits of Maya and Native American culture. "The Story of Man through the Ages" placed emphasis on the Indian populations of North and South America. San Diego is fortunate that many of the 1915 Exposition buildings survive— some have been restored and four reconstructed.

Twenty years later San Diego hosted a second exposition in Balboa Park. Within less than a year most of the 1915 Exposition buildings were repaired or remodeled for the 1935-1936 California Pacific International Exposition. Several new buildings were added around a Pan-American Plaza, with a singing fountain, along with the House of Pacific Relations, and Spanish Village. Top attractions included the Zoro Gardens Nudist Colony, the Midget Village, and Ripley's Believe-It-Or-Not. The Foreign Arts Building was remodeled as the House of Hospitality, much as we know it today, with its Casa del Rey Moro garden. A huge arch was placed in the middle of the Plaza de Panama, with shallow pools alongside. The 1935 Ford Building displayed automotive technology. In 1936 the 450 foot long *March of Transportation* mural (pages 72–73) was added, picturing modes of transportation used by humans since the days of the cave man through air travel and rocketry.

Both expositions were financially successful and helped boost San Diego's image.

Moorish tiles of dome of the San Diego Museum of Man and the California Tower

Mission bell adorns the House of Hospitality

Alcazar Garden replicates the palace courtyards of the Alcazar Castle in Seville, Spain. The garden features beautiful Moorish tile fountains and formal flowerbeds

Pages 10 and 11: Ornate entry doors of the San Diego Museum of Man
Bottom Left: The highly ornamental California Building and bell tower has been called the best example of Spanish baroque architecture in the world
Bottom Right: The California Tower of the San Diego Museum of Man seen from the Lawn Bowling greens

Huge Maya monuments, or stelae, in the Museum of Man rotunda, are from casts made for the 1915 Panama-California Exposition

Zuni and Hopi dolls

St Francis Chapel in the Museum of Man was designed for the 1915 Panama-California Exposition as an example of a Spanish Colonial church

Archways of the California Quadrangle adjacent to the Museum of Man

Following page: The formal rotunda of The San Diego Museum of Art

The highly ornamental façade of The San Diego Museum of Art is an example of the *platersque* style of architecture

Art of the 20th Century

French, Dutch, and Italian Art

Italian Renaissance Art

Art of the 20th Century

The Timken Museum of Art is considered one of the great small museums in the world, with the world-class Putnam Foundation Collection of European old master paintings, American paintings, and Russian Icons

The Casa de Balboa houses the Museum of Photographic Arts, the San Diego Model Railroad Museum, and the San Diego History Center

Painting, *Parable of the Sower*, by Pieter Brugel the elder (Timken Museum of Art)

Galleries of the Museum of Photographic Arts

Palm Canyon

A Moreton Bay Fig tree's sprawling root system can be found in Palm Canyon **Following page:** Mingei International Museum

The giant Bea Evenson fountain is the focal point of Fountain Plaza, adjacent to the NAT (San Diego Natural History Museum)

A view of the NAT's Atrium from Level 4 of the museum

Above: The San Diego Natural History Museum not only presents core and traveling exhibitions, but also has amassed a collection of more than 7 million specimens in its 140-year history
Bottom right: From dinosaurs to mastodons, travel through 75 million years and dig into the rich fossil history of Southern California and Baja California at the NAT's core exhibition, *Fossil Mysteries*

From beetles to bats, the NAT has more than 7 million in its research collection

The Reuben H. Fleet Science Center is a family favorite museum with a domed IMAX™ theater

Kid City is hands-on learning geared for toddlers

Spectacular IMAX™ films shown in the Heikoff Giant Dome Theater

Interactive exhibitions for children and adults are a Fleet favorite

TOP: Formed in 1948, San Diego Junior Theatre is the oldest youth theatre program in the United States

BOTTOM: The resident classical ballet school in Balboa Park, San Diego Civic Youth Ballet has held classes in the Casa del Prado since 1945

Civic Dance Arts, a program of the City of San Diego Park and Recreation Department, supports a premier dance program of high quality and affordable classes

San Diego Youth Symphony and Conservatory (SDYS) serves more than 600 students annually, from beginner to pre-professional

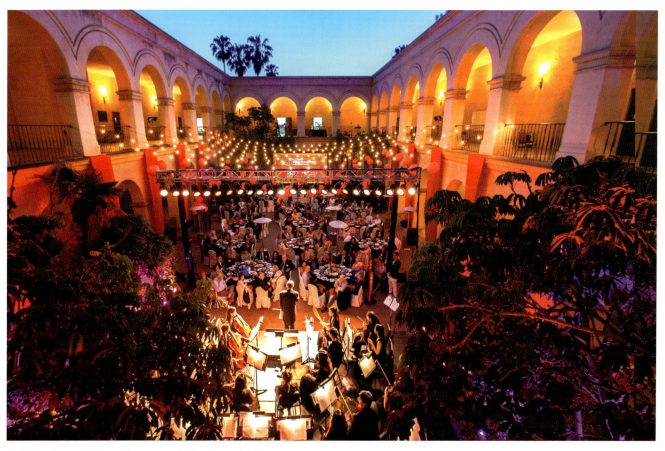
SDYS performs in the lovely courtyard of the Casa del Prado

Statues in the courtyard of Casa del Prado

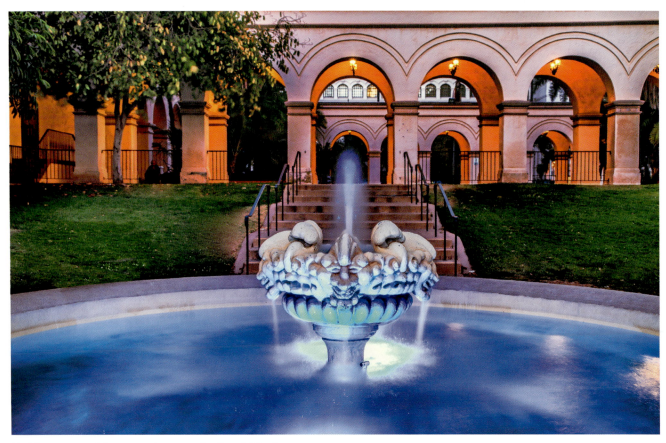
Highly ornamented fountains adjacent to the Casa del Prado

San Diego Floral Association and San Diego Botanical Garden Foundation

The Inez Grant Parker Memorial Rose Garden is ranked as one of the greatest public rose gardens in the world

Established in 1976, the Desert Garden contains more than 1,400 plants on 2.5 acres

Colorful flagstone patio of Spanish Village Art Center

The 1910 Balboa Park Carousel is a menagerie of animals. All but 2 pair are original

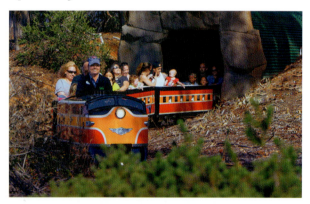
Owned and operated by the San Diego Zoo Department of Transportation, the Balboa Park Miniature Railroad takes a 3-minute, ½-mile trip through 4 acres of Balboa Park

Kids of all ages enjoy riding the historic Balboa Park Carousel

Daily art demonstrations featuring fine arts and crafts directly from San Diego's largest community of artists can be found at Spanish Village Art Center

3 museums, including the San Diego History Center, are located in the lovely Casa de Balboa

San Diego History Center

Casa de Balboa, 1915

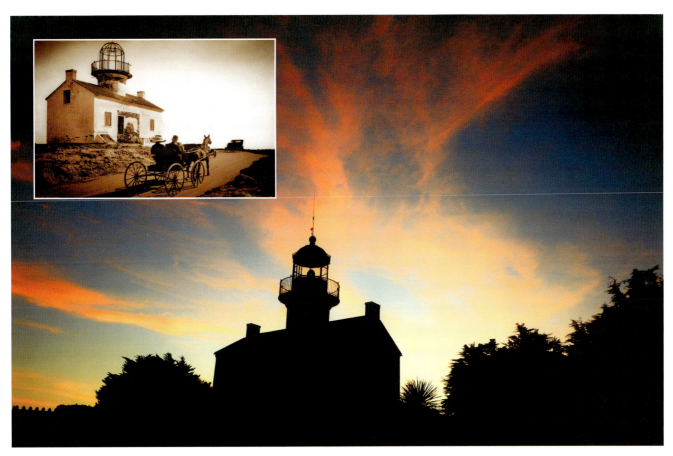

Point Loma Lighthouse, 1927 & present

Hotel Del Coronado, 1888 and present

Built for the 1915 Panama-California Exposition, the Botanical Building was one of the largest wood-lath structures in the world at that time, and was built at a cost of $53,386

More than 2,100 permanent plants can be found inside of the Botanical Building, including historic cycads, ferns, orchids, tropical plants, and palms

The Lily Pond, adjacent to the Botanical Building, was designed as a reflection pool, and contains water lilies and lotus that bloom May through October

St. Francis Chapel Bride

A señorita with mantilla and rose graces an intricately sculptured balcony

The internationally acclaimed, Tony Award®-winning Old Globe is one of the most esteemed regional theaters in the country

The spectacular House of Hospitality is located in the heart of Balboa Park

"The Woman of Tehuantepec" by artist Donal Hord, is the centerpiece of the House of Hospitality

Casa del Rey Moro Garden, designed for the 1935 California-Pacific Exposition, was influenced by the Moorish gardens of Rondo, Spain. Last year the garden was the scene of more than 440 weddings

El Prado

The main thoroughfare through the park

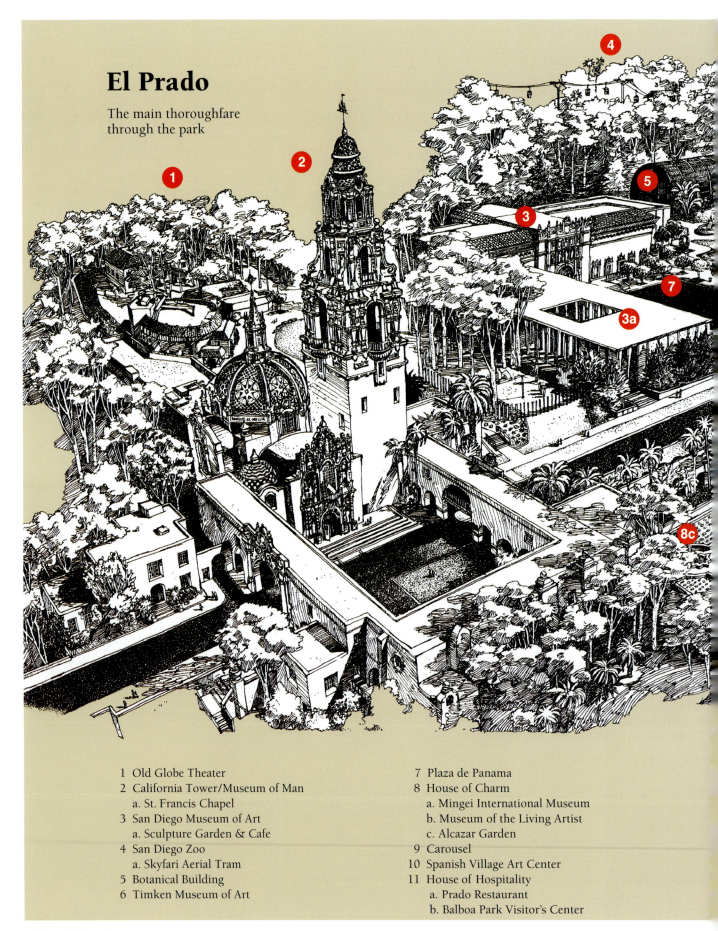

1. Old Globe Theater
2. California Tower/Museum of Man
   a. St. Francis Chapel
3. San Diego Museum of Art
   a. Sculpture Garden & Cafe
4. San Diego Zoo
   a. Skyfari Aerial Tram
5. Botanical Building
6. Timken Museum of Art
7. Plaza de Panama
8. House of Charm
   a. Mingei International Museum
   b. Museum of the Living Artist
   c. Alcazar Garden
9. Carousel
10. Spanish Village Art Center
11. House of Hospitality
    a. Prado Restaurant
    b. Balboa Park Visitor's Center

Map of Balboa Park

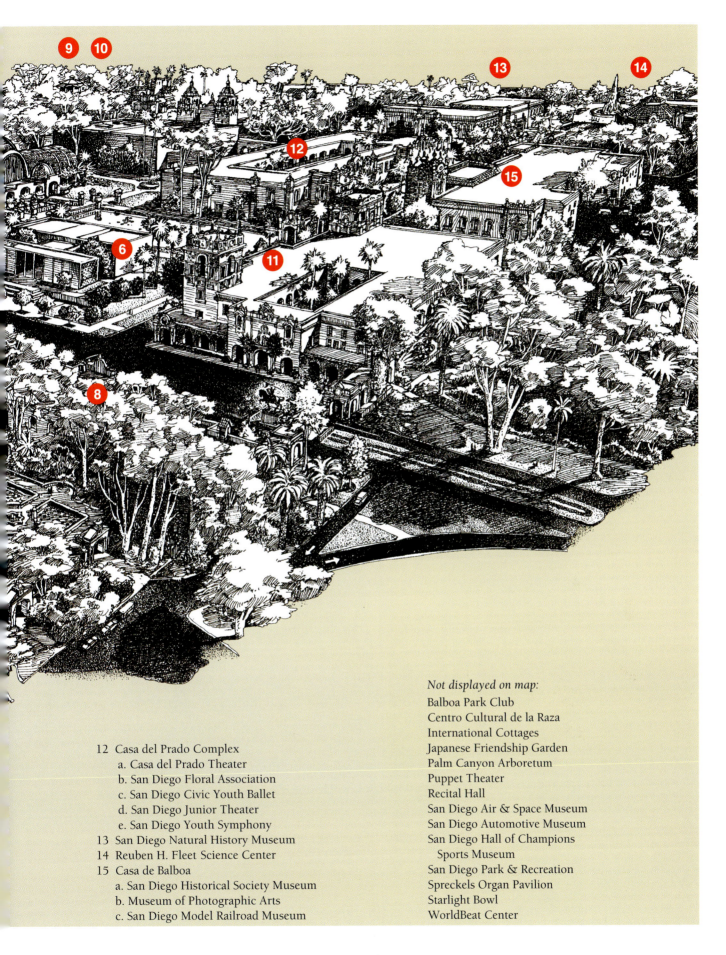

12 Casa del Prado Complex
   a. Casa del Prado Theater
   b. San Diego Floral Association
   c. San Diego Civic Youth Ballet
   d. San Diego Junior Theater
   e. San Diego Youth Symphony
13 San Diego Natural History Museum
14 Reuben H. Fleet Science Center
15 Casa de Balboa
   a. San Diego Historical Society Museum
   b. Museum of Photographic Arts
   c. San Diego Model Railroad Museum

Not displayed on map:
Balboa Park Club
Centro Cultural de la Raza
International Cottages
Japanese Friendship Garden
Palm Canyon Arboretum
Puppet Theater
Recital Hall
San Diego Air & Space Museum
San Diego Automotive Museum
San Diego Hall of Champions
   Sports Museum
San Diego Park & Recreation
Spreckels Organ Pavilion
Starlight Bowl
WorldBeat Center

Balboa Park December Nights is San Diego's largest free community festival and fills the Park with entertainment, free museums, food, and fabulous lights.

Santa and his reindeer greet revelers at Balboa Park December Nights

Peruvian dancers entertain at Balboa Park December Nights

Excerpts from San Diego Civic Youth Ballet's *The Nutcracker* can be seen during December Nights

The historic Botanical Building awash in holiday lights

San Diego Model Railroad Museum is one of the largest operating model railroad museums in the world

The Model Railroad Museum has 4 enormous scale and model layouts which depict railroads of the Southwest. The museum also features a Toy Train Gallery with an interactive Lionel layout for children

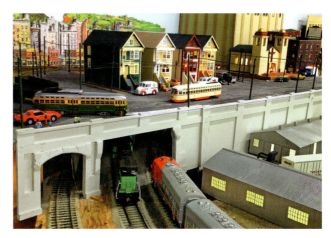

Quiet serenity of the Japanese Friendship Garden

The koi pond in the Japanese Friendship Garden is part of a typical *san-sui* (mountain and water) style garden with the waterfall reflecting the mountain, river, and ocean-scapes of the San Diego area and the turtle-shaped island in the pond symbolizing longevity

Meandering paths at the Japanese Friendship Garden take visitors through the largest cherry tree grove in San Diego

Spreckels Organ Pavilion and the elegant peristyles reflect the dream of John D. Spreckels to bring one of the world's largest outdoor pipe organs to the 1915 Panama-California Exposition. Since 1917 San Diego has had a civic organist who performs free weekly concerts on Sunday.

Following page: Housed in historic 1935 Exposition cottages, 32 groups promote multicultural goodwill and understanding through educational and cultural programs. Open Houses every Sunday, showcase the national traditions from many lands. Lawn programs feature music, dance, traditional costumes, arts, crafts, and ethnic foods.

Science, space, and aviation history all unfold at the San Diego Air & Space Museum which houses a collection of historic aircraft and spacecraft from all over the world

The Pavilion of Flight is the centerpiece of the San Diego Air and Space Museum

Ford 5-A-B-Trimotor displayed in the Pavilion of Flight

70

Mikoyan-Gurevich MiG-17 and McDonnell Douglas F-4J/S Phantom II

The "March of Transportation" was painted by Juan Larrinaga for the Ford Building at 1935 California-Pacific Exposition to depict the current vision of the past and future of transportation. As the largest mural in the western hemisphere it starts 12 feet off of the floor and continues 18 feet to the ceiling, and encircles the interior of the San Diego Air and Space Museum at 468 feet. (cont. pages 72 and 73)

The San Diego Hall of Champions Sports Museum is housed in the Federal Building, which was constructed for the 1935 California-Pacific Exposition

The Hall of Champions celebrates important moments in sporting history

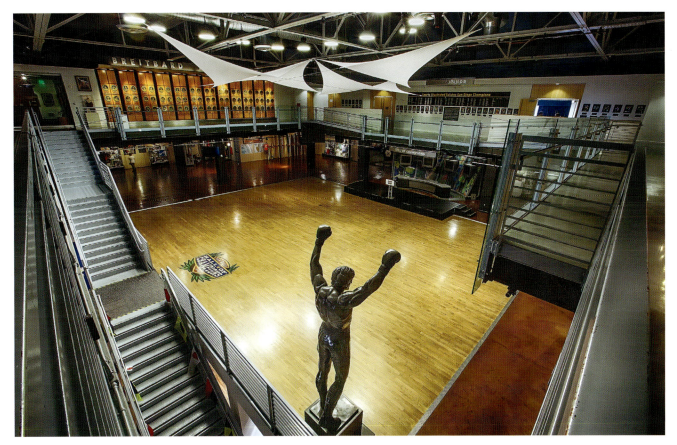
Center Court at the Hall of Champions

Sailing exhibit showcases a fully-rigged and previously raced Star class boat

The San Diego Automotive Museum houses more than 80 historic autos and motorcycles

1956 Chevrolet Nomad

1932 Cadillac V-12

1937 Lincoln-Zephyr V-12 Coupe

1939 Packard Super Touring

79

Housed in colorfully painted former water towers, WorldBeat Center and the Centro Cultural de la Raza celebrate international cultures. WorldBeat is dedicated to promoting and preserving African, African-American, and other indigenous cultures of the world through art, music, dance, and education; Centro preserves and educates about Chicano, Mexican, Indigenous and Latino art and cultures

The Veterans Museum and Memorial Center honors the memory of men and women of the Armed Forces, Coast Guard, and Wartime Merchant Marine

San Diego Art Institute (Museum of the Living Artist) showcases artists' works from the Southern California region

Millions of people enjoy the nearly 1,200 acres of Balboa Park. The Susan G. Koman Race for the Cure is an annual event; recreationists can bike in the Balboa Park Velodrome or swim in the Bud Kearns Memorial Pool at the Morley Field Sports Complex; or run, hike, or bike one of the many trails in Florida Canyon

Following page: Balboa Park's City golf course offers striking views of downtown San Diego and Coronado from many holes

A quiet footbridge in Marston Canyon
Below: The renowned horticulture of Balboa Park provides a colorful, fragrant, and serene environment

86

The Park's gorgeous horticulture inspires photographers

Redwood Circle is a little-known spot on the west mesa, with a majestic grove of Coast Redwood trees

Secluded pathways, including the Bridle Trail, can be found in the midst of this large urban park

Lemon-scented Gum Tree

Australian Tea Tree

Nate's Point off-leash dog park

There are nearly 15,000 trees in Balboa Park, of 350 different species

Following page: This classic 1905 Arts and Crafts style home, the Marston House and Garden was built for San Diego civic leader, George W. Marston, and is listed on the National Register of Historic Places

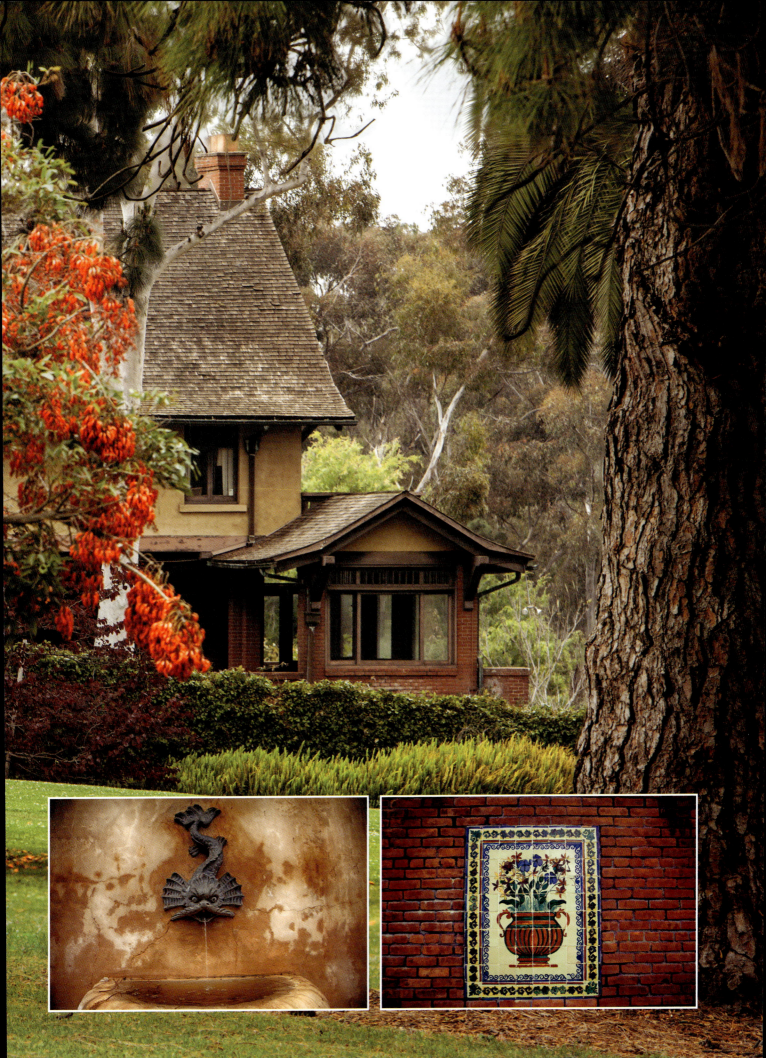

The San Diego Zoo is home to 3,700 rare and endangered animals. The more than 700,000 exotic plants in the Zoo's horticulture collection are often said to be more valuable than the animal collection

Following page: Mesmerizing and spectacular waterfall and landscaping at the Zoo's Gorilla Tropics

Produced and photographed by Richard Benton
Text: Mike Kelly/Debbie Petruzzelli
Design: Richard Benton/Alma Bell/John Pierce
Production Coordination: John Pierce
Composition: Alma Bell
Balboa Park Map: John Dawson
Special thank you: My mother—Eve Nelson; John Pierce; Todd Gloria, Mike Kelly, Debbie Petruzzelli
Dedicated to my wife Mavis, and others with breast cancer for their courageous fight against this devastating disease.
In memory of my friend Dr. Arlen Kantor

Photographic credits:
  Richard Benton: cover, inside back cover, back cover, 1; 6–100
  Benton Historical Collection: 2–3, inside front cover
  San Diego Historical Society: 1a; 4–5; 43 a–b
  Reuben H. Fleet Science Center: 29 top
  Old Globe Theatre: 48 top; Craig Schwartz

Thanks to:
Dawn Adams, Cisco Aguirre, Ellie Ambler, Roger Benton, Lucy Coker, Diane D'Angelo @ D'Angelo Designs, Brittany Darr, Andrea Feier, Steve and Janice Fitzgerald @ Prevue, Rex Garniewicz, Todd Gloria and Staff, Wendy Grant, Mohamad Hammad, Tom Hummel, Rosa Longacre, Marcy Melley, Danika Pramik-Holdaway, Michael Richards, Anthony Ridenhour, Brittany Saake, Suzanne Tawil-Betlach, April Tellez, Cris Travers, Sue Varga, Larry Vogel, Robert Von Klug, Cory Woodall, Jim Zuckerman

Library of Congress Control Number: 2014914651
ISBN 978-0-99067210-4   Hard cover

Library of Congress Control Number: 2014914651
ISBN 978-0-99067211-1   Paperback

Copyright 2014
To order additional books:
richardbenton@sbcglobal.net

Printed in China